this OR that?
weather

hurricane

OR

waterspout?

Josh Plattner

Consulting Editor, Diane Craig, M.A./Reading Specialist

Super Sandcastle

An Imprint of Abdo Publishing
abdopublishing.com

abdopublishing.com

Published by Abdo Publishing, a division of ABDO, PO Box 398166, Minneapolis, Minnesota 55439. Copyright © 2016 by Abdo Consulting Group, Inc. International copyrights reserved in all countries. No part of this book may be reproduced in any form without written permission from the publisher. Super SandCastle™ is a trademark and logo of Abdo Publishing.

Printed in the United States of America, North Mankato, Minnesota
102015
012016

Editor: Liz Salzmann
Content Developer: Nancy Tuminelly
Cover and Interior Design and Production: Mighty Media, Inc.
Photo Credits: Kelly Doudna, MISHELLA/Shutterstock NASA, NOAA, Shutterstock

Library of Congress Cataloging-in-Publication Data
Plattner, Josh, author.
  Hurricane or waterspout? / Josh Plattner ; consulting editor, Diane Craig.
    pages cm -- (This or that? Weather)
  ISBN 978-1-62403-955-3
1. Hurricanes--Juvenile literature. 2. Waterspouts--Juvenile literature. I. Craig, Diane, editor. II. Title.
  QC944.2.P53 2016
  551.55'2--dc23
                      2015021245

Super SandCastle™ books are created by a team of professional educators, reading specialists, and content developers around five essential components—phonemic awareness, phonics, vocabulary, text comprehension, and fluency—to assist young readers as they develop reading skills and strategies and increase their general knowledge. All books are written, reviewed, and leveled for guided reading and early reading intervention programs for use in shared, guided, and independent reading and writing activities to support a balanced approach to literacy instruction.

contents

hurricane or waterspout?

Is it a hurricane? Or is it a waterspout? Do you know the difference?

A hurricane is a storm. It forms over the ocean.

A waterspout is a **column** of air. It forms on water too.

by land or by sea?

Hurricanes begin in the open sea. Most form in the summer.

Waterspouts happen near the coast. They also happen in large lakes. The Great Lakes have waterspouts.

twisted types

Storms have wind. Sometimes the wind blows more than 74 miles per hour (119 kmh). It becomes a hurricane. The biggest hurricanes have winds stronger than 157 miles per hour (253 kmh)!

Some waterspouts
form in thunderstorms.
But most waterspouts
happen in fair weather.

wind and water

A hurricane forms over warm water. It forms near the **equator**. It forms where the winds are strong enough.

The earth turns. The turning causes air to spin. The spinning air becomes wind. The wind becomes a storm. The storm moves toward land.

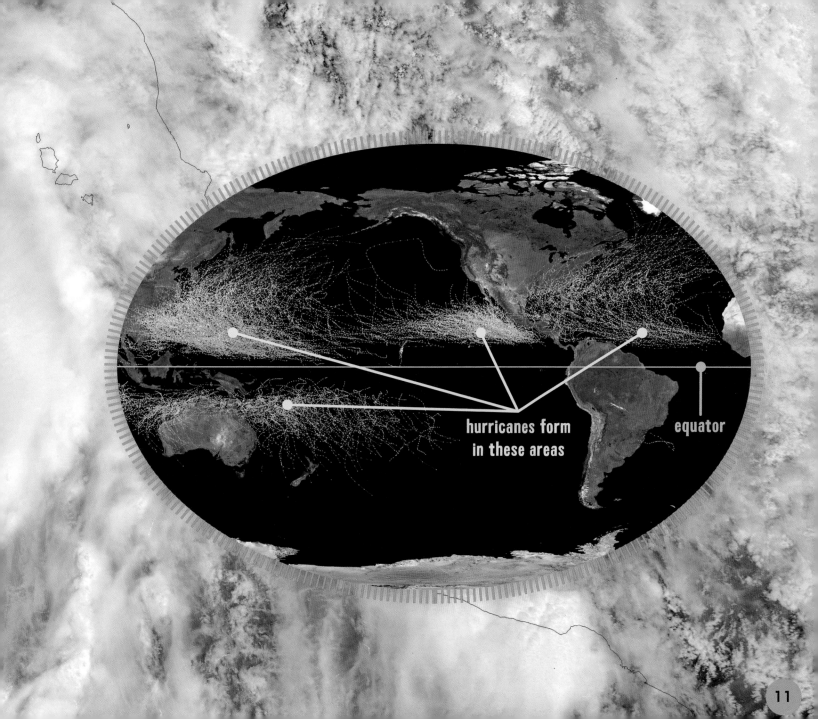

hurricanes form
in these areas

equator

A waterspout forms under a thick cloud. Warm air rises above the water from one spot. More air moves into that spot. The rising air spins.

The spinning air kicks up water drops. It carries the drops upward. The spinning air and water rises to the cloud.

water droplets rising
in the spinning air

storm sight

The middle of a
hurricane is clear.
This is the eye of the
storm. Clouds make a
wall around the eye.
Clouds move toward
the eye from far away.
The whole storm looks
like a giant **pinwheel**.

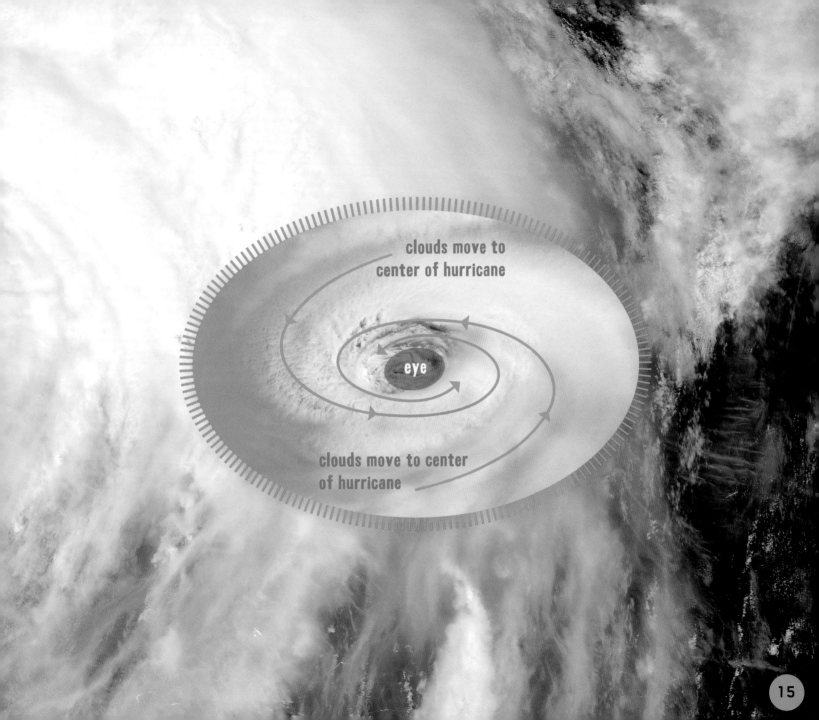

clouds move to center of hurricane

eye

clouds move to center of hurricane

A waterspout looks like a **column** of water. Wind spins around its center. But it is tiny compared to a hurricane.

More than one waterspout
can form. One area might
have three or four at once!

wind and water warning

High winds cause **damage** during a hurricane. The winds push big waves onto shore. This is a storm **surge**. The storm surge causes flooding. The flooding is unsafe.

Most waterspouts are weak. But they can **damage** boats and airplanes. They are unsafe for swimmers.

how long will this go on?

Hurricane-strength winds might last for only a few hours. Or they might last for many days. The storm itself can last for a week or more.

Waterspouts form and die quickly. They usually last less than 20 minutes.

at a glance

hurricane ——————— waterspout

forms over the ocean ——————— forms on coastal water

is a storm ——————— happens during fair weather

looks like a giant **pinwheel** ——————— looks like a **column** of water

has very strong winds ——————— does not have strong winds

can last for days ——————— lasts for a few minutes

tabletop hurricane

colorful swirls show how a hurricane spins.

What You'll Need
- large mixing bowl
- water
- large spoon
- food coloring

1 Fill the bowl with water.

2 Slowly stir the water with the spoon. Take the spoon out of the water.

3 Add two drops of food coloring.

4 Let the color **swirl** in the water.

think about it

How is the swirling color like a hurricane? Do you see a **pinwheel**? Do you see an eye?

glossary

column – a narrow pillar.

damage – harm or ruin.

equator – an imaginary line around the earth that is an equal distance from the north and south poles.

pinwheel – a light wheel that is attached to a stick so it can spin in the wind.

surge – a sudden, strong rush.

swirl – to whirl or to move smoothly in circles.